CLASS 08 LOCOMOTIVES

CW01619276

Andrew Cole

AMBERLEY

First published 2016

Amberley Publishing
The Hill, Stroud
Gloucestershire, GL5 4EP

www.amberley-books.com

Copyright © Andrew Cole, 2016

The right of Andrew Cole to be identified as the Author of this work has been asserted in accordance with the Copyrights, Designs and Patents Act 1988.

ISBN 978 1 4456 6208 4 (print)
ISBN 978 1 4456 6209 1 (ebook)

All rights reserved. No part of this book may be reprinted or reproduced or utilised in any form or by any electronic, mechanical or other means, now known or hereafter invented, including photocopying and recording, or in any information storage or retrieval system, without the permission in writing from the Publishers.

British Library Cataloguing in Publication Data.
A catalogue record for this book is available from the British Library.

Typesetting by Amberley Publishing.
Printed in the UK.

Introduction

A hundred Class 86 electric locomotives were built from 1965 onwards. The build was split between British Rail, who built forty at their Doncaster Works, and English Electric at their Vulcan Works, who built the remaining sixty. The class was originally designated as AL6, meaning they were the sixth design of the AC electric loco.

Built to a Bo-Bo bogie design, they were built for West Coast services from London Euston to Birmingham, Manchester and Liverpool. Later on, upon completion of the West Coast electrification, they would work further north to Glasgow. They helped oust steam and, later, the Class 50 diesel locomotives from the route.

The class was designated as the Class 86 under TOPS, and was numbered 86001 to 86048, and 86201 to 86252. The Class 86/0s were for freight work, whereas the Class 86/2s were for passenger workings. A further nine Class 86/0s were renumbered as Class 86/2s, bringing the passenger fleet up to sixty-one locos. Three Class 86/2s were fitted with different bogies that were intended for the Class 87s and were renumbered into the Class 86/1 series; these acted as test-bed locomotives for the Class 87.

Many members of the class were later fitted with TDM push-pull equipment to enable them to work with the MK3 driving van trailers for West Coast, helping eliminate the need for run round at terminal stations. Fifteen members of the class would later move to East Anglia for passenger workings from London Liverpool Street to Norwich, with these members passing to Anglia upon privatisation. They were later replaced on these services by Class 90s, which had become redundant on the West Coast with the introduction of the Pendolino EMUs. EWS found employment for another fifteen members of the class on parcels traffic and also for charter work, while Virgin Trains had over thirty members of the class for use on West Coast and cross-country services. Most were taken out of traffic in the early 2000s, going directly into storage. Freightliner also had a sizeable fleet of Class 86s and today are the largest operator of the class in the UK.

No. 86233 has since found its way to Bulgaria as a source of spares for the electric fleet in that country and, at the time of writing, another four members are due to follow. Floyd in Hungary also operates the class, having eight in use and one used as a source of spares. Four members of the class found their way into preservation, with Les Ross owning No. 86259, and the AC Locomotive Group owning the other three, although No. 86213 has been earmarked for export to Bulgaria as a spares loco.

All in all, the Class 86 has proved itself to be a very reliable and robust locomotive, with many surviving in use for over forty years, some now heading towards fifty years, and still giving sterling service both in the UK and in Europe.

No. 86001, 27 August 1985

No. 86001 (E3199) is seen stabled at Nuneaton while still painted in BR blue livery. This loco would later find fame when numbered as 86401, being the only member of the class to carry Network South East livery. It would go on to be named *Northampton Town*, and later *Mons Meg*.

No. 86004, 31 August 1984

No. 86004 (E3103) is seen stabled at Crewe along with No. 85031. The Class 86/0s were later renumbered into the Class 86/4 number series, and many were later renumbered into the Class 86/6 series when their ETH equipment was isolated, including No. 86004.

No. 86005, 2 April 1983

No. 86005 (E3185) rests at Cockshute sidings, Stoke-on-Trent. The Class 86/0s were fitted with multiple working cables on the cab front. This would eventually be renumbered 86605, and is still in use today with Freightliner – one of sixteen such locos still in use. This would later carry the name *Intercontainer*.

No. 86006, 20 August 1974

No. 86006 (E3112) is seen departing Birmingham New Street in the early 1970s, not long after being renumbered into the TOPS number series. No. 86006 would eventually be renumbered to 86606, and was withdrawn from use with Freightliner before being sent to Ron Hull Junior, Rotherham, for scrap. It was cut up in 2007.

No. 86008, 25 July 1975

No. 86008 (E3180) is seen stabled on one of the centre roads at Birmingham New Street while still carrying BR blue livery. This loco has carried many different numbers over the years, including 86408, 86608, 86501 before returning to 86608, which it carries today working for Freightliner.

No. 86010, 25 February 1984

No. 86010 (E3104) is seen undergoing overhaul at Crewe Works. Crewe undertook all the classified repairs to the AC electric fleet. No. 86610 is still in use today with Freightliner, carrying green livery.

No. 86027, 20 August 1974

No. 86027 (E3110) departs from Birmingham New Street with a passenger working to London Euston. This is another loco to go through various renumberings over the years, including 86327, 86427 and finally 86627, which it carries today working for Freightliner. This would go on to be named *The Industrial Society*.

No. 86030, 26 October 1982

No. 86030 (E3105) is seen at Nuneaton with a ballast working. The Class 86/0s were mainly used on freight workings; note how No. 86030 still retains the old-style pantograph in this view. This loco would eventually end up working for EWS on parcels traffic, before finally being scrapped by Booth Roe Metals, Rotherham, in 2005.

No. 86030, 22 March 1986

No. 86030 (E3105) passes through Crewe station with a rake of ICI tank wagons. Freight trains around Crewe normally used the freight avoiding lines round the back of the station. This would be named *Saint Edmund* when numbered 86430.

No. 86031, 1 January 1985

No. 86031 (E3188) spends New Year's Day 1985 stabled at Bescot, wearing BR blue livery. No. 86031 would eventually be renumbered to 86631, and was scrapped following collision damage it received at Stafford.

No. 86033, 10 August 1982

No. 86033 (E3198) is seen passing Rugby with a rake of domestic coal hoppers. The Class 86/0s were used mainly on freight work, and this was eventually renumbered as 86633, before finally being scrapped at Crewe L&NWR in 2013. This loco would carry the name *Wulfruna* when numbered 86433.

No. 86035, 27 August 1985

No. 86035 (E3124) is seen stabled at Nuneaton along with classmate No. 86001 and No. 20099. This siding has now been removed following the extension of the platforms. No. 86035 was renumbered 86435 before being renumbered again, this time to 86635, and was eventually scrapped at Crewe L&NWR in 2013.

No. 86036, 31 August 1984

No. 86036 (E3160) is seen passing the diesel depot at Crewe, coupled with classmate No. 86001. When used on freight work, the Class 86s were often run in pairs, which still happens today.

No. 86036, 1 January 1985

No. 86036 (E3160) is seen stabled at Bescot on New Year's Day 1985. No. 86036 would eventually be renumbered 86636, and was scrapped by Booth Roe Metals, Rotherham, in 2005.

No. 86037, 23 November 1985

No. 86037 (E3130) departs Crewe with a passenger working, bound for London Euston. Note the loco still retains the old-style pantograph in this photograph.

No. 86037, 31 March 1986

No. 86037 (E3130) is seen stabled at Bescot, complete with lowered pantograph. This loco is still in use today, carrying Freightliners new PowerHaul livery, and is one of two locos to carry the livery, No. 86622 being the other.

No. 86101, 31 August 1984

No. 86101 (E3191) *Sir William A Stanier F.R.S.* is seen stabled at Crewe before the station was remodelled. This view shows the Class 87-style bogies fitted to the Class 86/1s. No. 86101 is still in use today, having been preserved by the AC Locomotive Group, and is used on overnight Caledonian Sleeper workings.

No. 86101, 29 August 1989

No. 86101 (E3191) *Sir William A Stanier F.R.S.* is seen making a station call at Nuneaton, while carrying InterCity livery. At the time the loco had the really small running numbers, but these were replaced.

No. 86101, 24 April 2015

No. 86101 (E3191) *Sir William A Stanier F.R.S.* is seen at London Euston carrying Caledonian Sleeper livery, having brought the empty stock in for the overnight sleeper. This loco is owned by the AC Locomotive Group.

No. 86103, 31 August 1984

No. 86103 (E3143) *Andre Chapelon* departs Crewe while wearing BR blue livery. There were only three members of the Class 86/1 sub class, and they were all fitted with Class 87 bogies.

No. 86103, 29 March 1991

No. 86103 (E3143) *Andre Chapelon* arrives at Birmingham International while on a passenger working. Note that the first carriage is painted in Trans Pennine livery. No. 86103 would eventually be scrapped at Immingham in 2002.

No. 86204, 17 March 1983

No. 86204 (E3173) *City of Carlisle* is seen running into one of the centre roads at Birmingham New Street to stable, having brought a passenger working in from the north. No. 86204 would eventually be scrapped at Immingham in 2003.

No. 86205, 6 March 2002

No. 86205 (E3129) *City of Lancaster* is seen making a station call at Stafford while on a Virgin Trains working. Note the three plaques above the nameplate.

No. 86205, 8 February 2003

No. 86205 (E3129) *City of Lancaster* is seen at Birmingham International while propelling a Virgin Trains working from Birmingham New Street to London Euston. No. 86205 was eventually renumbered 86701, and had previously carried the number 86503.

No. 86206, 29 March 1991

No. 86206 (E3184) *City of Stoke-On-Trent* makes the station call at Birmingham International while working to London Euston. Note the parcels liveried BG behind the loco, in the absence of a MK3 DVT.

No. 86206, 28 May 1998

No. 86206 (E3184) *City of Stoke-on-Trent* departs Crewe with a southbound Virgin Trains working while still carrying InterCity Swallow livery. No. 86206 would be scrapped by Sims McIntyre Recycling, Cardiff, in 2004.

No. 86207, 1 June 1981

No. 86207 (E3179) *City of Lichfield* makes the station call at Nuneaton, having arrived from London Euston. This had only been named three months previously. This would be scrapped by Ron Hull, Rotherham, in 2006.

No. 86207, 14 February 1987

No. 86207 (E3179) *City of Lichfield* departs Crewe with a southbound passenger working while still carrying BR blue livery.

No. 86207, 6 August 1990

No. 86207 (E3179) *City of Lichfield* is seen stabled at London Euston, waiting for its next turn of duty. The loco carries the small running numbers, which were thankfully replaced.

No. 86208, 18 January 1986

No. 86208 (E3141) *City of Chester* is seen at Birmingham New Street carrying the original InterCity livery. This was the first Class 86 to be built by English Electric at their Vulcan Works.

No. 86208, 24 May 1990

No. 86208 (E3141) *City of Chester* arrives at Birmingham International with a working from London Euston. This loco would be scrapped at Crewe in 2003.

No. 86208, 30 August 1996

No. 86208 (E3141) *City of Chester* is seen stabled at Glasgow Central. At this time the loco worked for RES and carries a small logo above the running number. It has had the InterCity branding removed.

No. 86209, 24 May 1998

No. 86209 (E3125) *City of Coventry* stands at Crewe, carrying InterCity Swallow livery, with a working to Manchester Piccadilly.

No. 86209, 6 October 2003

No. 86209 (E3125) *City of Coventry* passes through Bethnal Green with an Anglia working from Norwich to London Liverpool Street. This had recently moved to Norwich and still carries former operator Virgin Trains' livery. This loco was eventually scrapped by S. Wheeler, Boreham in 2005.

No. 86210, 22 October 1996

No. 86210 (E3190) *C.I.T. 75th Anniversary* departs Darlington with a rake of parcels vans while carrying Rail Express Systems livery. RES had a small stud of electric loco for such workings. This was renumbered 86902 in 2004 and found use with Network Rail. This loco also carried the name *City of Edinburgh*.

No. 86211, 26 October 1982

86211 (E3147) *City of Milton Keynes* stands at Nuneaton with a rake of MK3 carriages. This loco was one of two Class 86 locos written off and scrapped following the Colwich accident in 1986. Note it still carries the BR double arrow on the cab side.

No. 86211, 22 March 1986

No. 86211 (E3147) *City of Milton Keynes* is seen waiting to depart from Crewe with a passenger working to the south. This was scrapped at Crewe Works in 1987 following collision damage received in the Colwich accident.

No. 86212, 8 February 1999

No. 86212 (E3151) *Preston Guild 1328–1992* arrives at Birmingham New Street while carrying InterCity Swallow livery. This name on the loco used to just say *Preston Guild*, the dates being added in 1992.

No. 86212, 7 June 2009

No. 86212 (E3151) is seen in long-term storage at MOD Long Marston. At this time there were large numbers of AC electric locos stored here. No. 86212 would go to EMR Kingsbury for scrap in 2011.

No. 86213, 12 April 1986

No. 86213 (E3193) *Lancashire Witch* is seen stabled at Bescot while still carrying BR blue livery.

No. 86213, 20 August 1993

No. 86213 (E3193) *Lancashire Witch* makes the station call at Stafford with an InterCity working to Manchester Piccadilly. This loco was saved for preservation, but has since been sold for export to Bulgaria for spare parts.

No. 86215, 18 January 1986

No. 86215 (E3165) *Joseph Chamberlain* departs from Birmingham New Street while heading towards London Euston. The loco still carries BR blue livery, but the coaching stock has been repainted into InterCity livery. This loco has carried several different names, including *Norwich Cathedral, Norfolk & Norwich Festival* and *The Round Tabler*.

No. 86215, 7 September 2004

No. 86215 (E3165) *The Round Tabler* is seen passing through Bethnal Green on the back of an Anglia service to Norwich. The train is being propelled by the loco with a MK2 DVT leading.

No. 86215, 7 June 2009

No. 86215 (E3165) *The Round Tabler* is seen in Anglia livery while in long-term storage at MOD Long Marston. This was later taken out of storage, refurbished for Floyd and exported to Hungary.

No. 86217, 9 June 2007

No. 86217 (E3177) leads a line of other stored Class 86s at MOD Long Marston. This loco was later refurbished for Floyd and was exported to Hungary, one of eight so treated. Another was exported for spares. This is another loco to have carried various names, including *Comet*, *Halley's Comet* and *City University*.

No. 86218, 3 September 1994

No. 86218 (E3175) *Harold Macmillan* is seen in storage inside Springburn Works, Glasgow. The loco carries InterCity Swallow livery and would be repaired and returned to traffic at Norwich. It was later sold to Floyd, and currently works in Hungary.

No. 86218, 9 September 2002

No. 86218 (E3175) *NHS 50* is seen at Norwich, waiting to depart for London Liverpool Street. The loco carries Anglia livery, and would be sold to Floyd for use in Hungary. The Norwich-based Class 86s always seemed to carry different names at some point, including No. 86218, which has carried the names *Planet, Harold MacMillan, Year of Opera & Musical Theatre 1997* and *NHS 50*.

No. 86219, 31 August 1996

No. 86219 (E3196) *Phoenix* is seen withdrawn at Springburn Works, Glasgow. This loco had been in storage and would never turn a wheel in service again, being scrapped at Immingham in 2002.

No.86220, 10 March 1988

No. 86220 (E3156) *The Round Tabler* is seen working south through Adderley Park, in the Birmingham suburbs, with an InterCity working to London Euston. Of note is the blue-and-grey BG included in the consist in place of the Mk3 DVT. No. 86220 would eventually be scrapped at Immingham in 2003. No. 86220 was originally named *Goliath*.

No. 86222, 3 April 1985

No. 86222 (E3131) *Fury* is seen waiting departure from Nuneaton with an express working to the north. This loco would lose the name *Fury*, becoming *Lloyds List 250th Anniversary*, but would end up being named *Clothes Show Live*.

No. 86222, 29 March 1991

No. 86222 (E3131) *Lloyds List 250th Anniversary* is seen at Birmingham International running light engine. The loco carries InterCity Swallow livery. This loco also carried the number 86502 for a short while when it was used as a freight loco.

No. 86222, 16 June 2000

No. 86222 (E3131) *Clothes Show Live* is seen at Carlisle waiting to depart with a Cross Country working to the south. The loco carries Virgin Trains livery, but the carriages still retain their InterCity colours. This would be scrapped at Immingham in 2003.

No. 86223, 7 June 2009

No. 86223 (E3158) is seen in long-term storage at MOD Long Marston while carrying Anglia livery. The loco had lost its *Norwich Union* name by this time and would be scrapped at EMR Kingsbury in 2011. It had originally been named *Hector*.

No. 86224, 17 May 1997

No. 86224 (E3134) *Caledonian* is seen having arrived at London Euston with an early morning arrival from Birmingham New Street. The loco carries InterCity Swallow livery.

No. 86224, 28 May 1998

No. 86224 (E3134) is seen making a station call at Stafford with a Virgin Trains CrossCountry working to Manchester Piccadilly. At this time No. 86224 was running round without a name. This would be scrapped by Ron Hull, Rotherham.

No. 86225, 14 February 1988

No. 86225 (E3164) *Hardwicke* is seen stabled at Bescot along with a Class 85. No. 86225 carries original InterCity livery and would eventually be scrapped by Ron Hull, Rotherham in 2005.

No. 86226, 10 May 1996

No. 86226 (E3162) *Charles Rennie Mackintosh* is seen at Birmingham New Street just two days after being named. The loco carries InterCity livery and is still in a very respectable condition following the naming. This had originally been named *Mail*, before carrying the name *Royal Mail Midlands*.

No. 86226, 26 May 1998

No. 86226 (E3162) *Charles Rennie Mackintosh* is seen stabled on one of the centre roads at Liverpool Lime Street, while a waiting its next turn of duty. This would eventually be scrapped by EMR Kingsbury in 2011.

No. 86227, 1 June 1996

No. 86227 (E3117) *Sir Henry Johnson* is seen departing a sunny Crewe with an InterCity CrossCountry service towards Birmingham New Street. This would be scrapped by Ron Hull, Rotherham, in 2005. It had also carried the name *Golden Jubilee*.

No. 86228, 7 June 2009

No. 86228 (E3167) *Vulcan Heritage* is seen in long-term storage at MOD Long Marston while carrying InterCity Swallow livery, but with the logos removed. This was eventually refurbished and was exported to Hungary, working for Floyd.

No. 86229, 29 March 1991

86229 (E3119) *Sir John Betjeman* is seen at Birmingham International while carrying InterCity livery. The loco is seen propelling, with a Mk3 DVT leading from the front, but unusually the consist includes a Mk2 brake vehicle. It would lose its name in 1998, becoming *Lions Club International*.

No. 86230, 9 September 2002

No. 86230 (E3168) is seen propelling a rake of MK2 carriages out of Ipswich while carrying Anglia livery. At this time the loco was running round nameless, having been previously been named *The Duke of Wellington*, and would eventually be scrapped by EMR Kingsbury in 2011.

No.86230, 6 October 2003

No. 86230 (E3168) passes Bethnal Green with an Anglia working towards London Liverpool Street. The loco carries Anglia livery and, at this time, had lost its name *The Duke of Wellington*. No. 86230 would be scrapped by EMR Kingsbury in 2011.

No. 86231, 3 April 1986

No. 86231 (E3126) *Starlight Express* is seen carrying original InterCity livery at London Euston with BR blue No. 86245 in the background. No. 86231 would eventually pass to Virgin Trains before going into long-term storage at MOD Long Marston.

No. 86231, 7 June 2009

No. 86231 (E3126) stands among many other withdrawn Class 86s at MOD Long Marston. The best of the stored fleet were refurbished for Floyd and exported to Hungary, but No. 86231 was never refurbished.

No. 86233, 27 August 1985

No. 86233 (E3172) *Laurence Olivier* is seen carrying BR blue livery while making a station call at Nuneaton. It would go on to be named *Alstom Heritage*, and this loco would eventually be exported to Bulgaria as a source of spare parts for the Class 87s that were exported out there.

No. 86233, 28 May 1998

No. 86233 (E3172) *Laurence Olivier* stands at Stafford with a Virgin Trains CrossCountry working to Manchester Piccadilly. The loco still carries InterCity Swallow livery at this time, and would gain fame later on by being repainted back into the original blue livery.

No. 86233, 14 July 2003

No. 86233 (E3172) *Alstom Heritage* is seen waiting to depart from London Euston with a Virgin Trains West Coast working to Birmingham New Street. This loco had been superbly repainted back into its original livery and would carry it until it was exported to Bulgaria to act as a source of spare parts.

No. 86233, 7 June 2009

No. 86233 (E3172) stands at MOD Long Marston in long-term storage. This had been repainted by Virgin Trains back into its original livery, and in this view it had lost both its name, *Alstom Heritage,* and the BR lion and wheel. It would later be exported to Bulgaria to act as a source of spare parts for the Class 87 fleet that operate over there. It had originally been named *Laurence Olivier.*

No. 86234, 1 May 1993

No. 86234 (E3155) *J.B. Priestly O.M.* is seen inside Springburn Works, Glasgow, while undergoing a classified overhaul. It would emerge still carrying InterCity Swallow livery. It would also carry the name *Suffolk – Relax, Refresh, Return.*

No. 86234, 21 September 1995

No. 86234 (E3155) *J.B. Priestly O.M.* is seen running light engine out of Manchester Piccadilly, having brought an InterCity working in. This loco later moved to Anglia, being based at Norwich.

No. 86234, 7 June 2009

No. 86234 (E3155) is seen carrying Anglia livery while in long-term storage at MOD Long Marston. The Class 86s based at Norwich had been replaced by ex-Virgin Trains Class 90s. No. 86234 is expected to be exported to Bulgaria as a source of spare parts. This loco had carried the names *J.B. Priestly O.M.* and *Suffolk – Relax, Refresh, Return.*

No. 86235, 18 August 1980

No. 86235 (E3194) *Novelty* is seen at the now-demolished Vauxhall carriage sidings, near Duddeston, Birmingham. The loco carries a special livery commemorating the fact that it had been used in the Rainhill cavalcade earlier in the year. This loco has been sold for spare parts, and will be exported to Bulgaria.

No. 86235, 7 September 2004

No. 86235 (E3194) *Crown Point* is seen passing Bethnal Green on the back of an Anglia working from London Liverpool Street to Norwich. The loco carries Anglia livery and has recently been sold for export to Bulgaria to act as a source of spares. This loco also carried the names *Novelty* and *Harold MacMillan*.

No. 86235, 29 December 2015

No. 86235 (E3194) is seen at Leicester carrying Anglia livery. This loco has been in long-term storage for a number of years and has now been sold for export to Bulgaria to act as a source of spare parts.

No. 86236, 22 April 1987

No. 86236 (E3133) *Josiah Wedgwood Master Potter 1730-1795* approaches Nuneaton while heading south towards London Euston. The loco carries original InterCity livery and would later be scrapped at Immingham in 2003.

Nos 86236 and 86225, 18 August 1997

No. 86236 (E3133) *Josiah Wedgwood Master Potter 1730–1795* is seen at London standing next to No. 86225 (E3164) *Hardwicke*, both having arrived with InterCity services from the north. Both locos have since been scrapped.

No. 86236, 26 January 2001

No. 86236 (E3133) *Josiah Wedgwood Master Potter 1730–1795* is seen stabled underneath Birmingham New Street signal box while carrying Virgin Trains livery. Today these sidings are no longer used, and the loco has been scrapped.

No. 86237, 11 May 2001

No. 86237 (E3197) *University of East Anglia* is seen at Colchester. The loco carries Anglia livery and would eventually be scrapped by Sims Metals in 2004. This had originally been named *Sir Charles Halle.*

No. 86239, 23 July 1985

No. 86239 (E3169) *L.S. Lowry* is seen at London Liverpool Street while still carrying BR blue livery. This loco was renumbered 86507 for a short while before reverting back to 86239, and was unfortunately involved in the Rickerscote accident in 1996. It was scrapped at Crewe Electric depot in 1997.

Nos 86239 and 90024, 20 August 1993

No. 86239 (E3169) *L.S. Lowry* is seen hauling Railfreight Speedlink-liveried No. 90024 through Crewe station. No. 86239 carries parcels red livery and would be scrapped within four years time following collision damage received at Rickerscote.

No. 86240, 24 May 1998

No. 86240 (E3127) *Bishop Eric Treacy* is seen arriving at Crewe station with a rake of InterCity-liveried MK2 carriages. No. 86240 later received Virgin Trains livery and was scrapped by Ron Hull, Rotherham, in 2005.

No. 86240, 17 January 2002

No. 86240 (E3127) *Bishop Eric Treacy* is seen making a station call at Stafford while carrying Virgin Trains red livery. This would be scrapped by Ron Hull, Rotherham, in 2005.

No. 86241, 25 October 1993

No. 86241 (E3121) *Glenfiddich* is seen at Crewe station carrying parcels red livery. It is seen hauling the Crewe Works test train, which consisted of various redundant carriages, including a Mk2 FO.

No. 86241, 25 October 1996

No. 86241 (E3121) *Glenfiddich* is seen approaching Doncaster carrying Rail Express Systems red livery. The loco is on Railtour duty, heading for the north. No. 86241 was eventually scrapped at Crewe Electric depot in 2003.

No. 86242, 31 August 1984

No. 86242 (E3138) *James Kennedy G.C.* is seen at Crewe station while at the head of a Travelling Post Office working. This was one of the first AC electric locos to carry InterCity livery, and was very different from the standard BR blue that was applied to everything at the time. It would later be named *Colchester Castle*.

No. 86242, 6 June 1997

No. 86242 (E3138) *James Kennedy G.C.* is seen passing through Rugby with a rake of InterCity-liveried Mk2 carriages. No. 86242 was eventually refurbished after a period in store, and was exported to Hungary for use with Floyd.

No. 86244, 10 June 1999

No. 86244 (E3178) *The Royal British Legion* is seen approaching Warrington Bank Quay with a rake of Virgin Trains-liveried carriages. No. 86244 was scrapped at Immingham in 2003.

No. 86245, 3 April 1985

No. 86245 (E3182) *Dudley Castle* pauses at Nuneaton, carrying BR blue livery. This would go on to be a celebrity later in life by carrying Virgin Trains livery, but the red was replaced with blue, and it carried the name *Caledonian*. It was scrapped by EMR Kingsbury in 2010.

No. 86246, 31 August 1984

No. 86246 (E3149) is seen stabled at Crewe before the station was remodelled. At this time the loco was not named, but would later carry *Royal Anglian Regiment* plates, and is still around today carrying Anglia livery. It is stored at Willesden.

No. 86247, 18 January 1986

No. 86247 (E3192) *Abraham Darby* is seen departing Birmingham New Street with an InterCity working for London Euston. This loco was stored for a number of years at MOD Long Marston before it was refurbished for Europhoenix and used as a demonstrator loco, but was sold for scrap, being cut up in 2015 at Crewe Basford Hall.

No. 86247, 22 April 1996

No. 86247 (E3192) *Abraham Darby* is seen stabled at Liverpool Lime Street while carrying InterCity Swallow livery. This livery really suited the Class 86s.

No. 86247, 7 June 2009

No. 86247 (E3192) is seen on display at MOD Long Marston. The loco carries Europhoenix livery, and was used as a demonstrator loco, due to the fact that there were so many Class 86s in storage. The loco was eventually scrapped at Crewe Basford Hall yard in 2015.

No. 86248, 15 September 1989

No. 86248 (E3107) *Sir Clwyd/County of Clwyd* passes through Adderley Park in the Birmingham suburbs with a parcels working. The loco carries InterCity mainline livery. It would eventually be refurbished for export,and can be found in Hungary working for Floyd.

No. 86248, 7 February 2009

No. 86248 (E3107) is seen at the L&NWR carriage sidings at Crewe. The loco carries the livery of Hungarian operator Floyd and was later exported, one of eight such locos.

No. 86249, 24 May 1998

No. 86249 (E3161) *County of Merseyside* is seen approaching Crewe with an InterCity working. The loco carries Swallow livery and would eventually be scrapped at MOD Caerwent in 2005.

No. 86249, 6 March 2002

No. 86249 (E3161) *County of Merseyside* is seen arriving at Stafford with a Virgin Trains CrossCountry working to the south. This was one of the few Virgin operated Class 86s that never received their livery.

No. 86250, 5 September 1989

No. 86250 (E3189) *The Glasgow Herald* is seen arriving at Birmingham New Street with an InterCity working. The loco carries InterCity mainline livery, which was a favourite livery of mine – especially with the red buffer beam and the black headcode box. It would later be named *Sheppard 100*.

No. 86250, 9 September 2002

No. 86250 (E3189) is seen at Norwich carrying Anglia livery during the period when it was not named. It would later carry the name *Sheppard 100*. After a period in store, it was refurbished for Floyd and exported to Hungary.

No. 86251, 1 June 1996

No. 86251 (E3183) *The Birmingham Post* departs Crewe propelling an InterCity working south towards London Euston. A few members of the class were named after regional newspapers, including No. 86251. This loco is at MOD Long Marston for spares and is expected to be scrapped.

No. 86253, 2 June 1984

No. 86253 (E3136) *The Manchester Guardian* is seen departing Crewe in a classic 1980s BR-blue period photograph. This would be refurbished for Network Rail and was renumbered 86901. It is currently at CF Booths, Rotherham for spares recovery before final scrapping.

No. 86253, 14 September 1989

No. 86253 (E3136) *The Manchester Guardian* is seen approaching Adderley Park, just outside Birmingham New Street, with an InterCity working from London Euston. This loco was converted into a mobile load bank loco and was renumbered 86901.

No. 86253, 6 June 1997

No. 86253 (E3136) *The Manchester Guardian* is seen stabled at Rugby carrying InterCity Swallow livery. These two north bays have since been lifted and the impressive roof has been removed.

No. 86254, 18 March 1997

No. 86254 (E3142) is seen approaching Thirsk on the East Coast main line with a southbound parcels working. The loco carries Rail Express Systems livery, and was one of a small stud of locos used by EWS on parcels workings. This was eventually scrapped by Booth Roe Metals, Rotherham, in 2004. It had once been named *William Webb Ellis*.

No. 86256, 31 July 1982

No. 86256 (E3135) *Pebble Mill* is seen at Birmingham New Street carrying BR blue livery. This time period was how I best remember the Class 86s, in blue livery with matching blue-and-grey coaches. No. 86256 was eventually scrapped by Ron Hull Junior, Rotherham, in 2006.

No. 86256, 17 March 1983

No. 86256 (E3135) *Pebble Mill* is seen stabled on one of the centre roads at Birmingham New Street while carrying BR blue livery.

No. 86256, 29 December 1991

No. 86256 (E3135) *Pebble Mill* is seen approaching Bescot with an InterCity working. This loco was eventually scrapped by Ron Hull Junior, Rotherham, in 2006.

Nos 86256 and 87007, 11 August 1997

No. 86256 (E3135) *Pebble Mill* is seen at London Euston alongside No. 87007 *City of Manchester*. This view shows the two different front ends carried by the two classes. No. 86256 was later scrapped, while No. 87007 was exported to Bulgaria following the introduction of the Class 390 Pendolino units on the West Coast.

No. 86257, 1 May 1993

No. 86257 (E3139) *Snowdon* is seen inside Springburn Works, Glasgow, receiving a classified repair. The overhaul has included a repaint into InterCity Swallow livery. No. 86257 would be scrapped at Immingham in 2003.

No. 86258, 7 June 2009

No. 86258 (E3140) is seen in long-term storage at MOD Long Marston. The loco unusually carries plain orange livery, following a controlled collision with a MK2 carriage. No. 86258 was the last Class 86 to be built at BR Doncaster Works, and it was scrapped by EMR Kingsbury in 2009. This once carried the name *Talyllyn – The First Preserved Railway*, only to have the plates changed to *Talyllyn 50 Years of Railway Preservation 1951-2001*.

No. 86259, 14 January 2007

No. 86259 (E3137) *Les Ross* is seen at Tyseley having been preserved. This loco has been returned to as near original condition as possible, and carries the name of its new owner. The finish on this loco is superb, and is main-line-registered for charter and special workings. This was originally named *Peter Pan* and has also carried the name *Greater Manchester The Life & Soul of Britain*.

No. 86260, 23 November 1985

No. 86260 (E3144) *Driver Wallace Oakes G.C.* is seen inside the paint shop at Crewe Works, having been rubbed down ready for a repaint from BR blue livery to InterCity livery. Note how the position of the nameplate has moved from the centre of the bodyside to further up the left. No. 86260 would eventually carry the number 86702 when it was used by Electric Traction Limited.

No. 86260, 22 April 1987

No. 86260 (E3144) *Driver Wallace Oakes G.C.* powers south through Nuneaton with an InterCity working to London Euston. The loco carries original InterCity livery and has received the TDM cables on the front to allow it to work with a MK3 DVT on these workings.

No. 86260, 30 August 1996

No.86260 (E3144) *Driver Wallace Oakes G.C.* is seen at Carlisle waiting to depart with a CrossCountry working towards Birmingham New Street. Driver Wallace Oakes suffered burns when in charge of a steam working at Winsford, staying with the loco to apply the brakes. He later died from his injuries and was awarded the George Cross; and No. 86260 was named after him.

No. 86260, 7 June 2009

No. 86260 (E3144) is seen at MOD Long Marston. The loco has been refurbished, carries the livery of Electric Traction Limited and, when released from Long Marston, had been renumbered to 86702. This loco has recently been sold and will be exported to Bulgaria as a source of spare parts for the fleet of AC electrics in use over there.

No. 86261, 27 March 1993

No. 86261 (E3118) is seen inside the shed at Crewe Electric depot. The loco carries Rail Express Systems livery, and was one of a small batch of Class 86s that were used on parcels traffic. It was later sold to EWS for the same use and was eventually scrapped by Booth Roe Metals, Rotherham, in 2004. This had once been named *Driver John Axon GC*. Driver Axon was awarded the George Cross after trying to stop a runaway freight train at Chapel-en-le-Frith.

No. 86316, 14 August 1982

No. 86316 (E3109) is seen stabled on one of the centre roads at Birmingham New Street. The loco is still in pretty much original condition, with original bogies, without the flexicoil suspension and pantograph. Note the addition of the small headlight. This would go on to be renumbered No. 86416 and work for Rail Express Systems, and would be named *Wigan Pier* when numbered 86416.

No. 86316, 13 December 1986

No. 86316 (E3118) is seen inside Crewe Works undergoing classified repair. The repair would include the fitting of new suspension, and repainting into InterCity livery. When released from overhaul it would emerge as No. 86416 and would be named *Wigan Pier*.

No. 86318, 9 March 1985

No. 86318 (E3163) is seen stabled at Bescot carrying BR blue livery. This view shows the original bogies fitted to the class before the flexicoil suspension was added to improve the ride of these locos. This loco would go on to be renumbered 86418, and finally 86618.

No. 86318, 3 April 1985

No. 86318 (E3163) stands at Nuneaton with an InterCity working northwards. This view shows the multiple working cables and sockets on the front, which were fitted to many members of the class.

No. 86324, 2 June 1984

No. 86324 (E3111) departs from Crewe with a southbound passenger working. No. 86324 still carries its BR double arrow in the centre of the bodyside and doesn't carry the multiple working cables and sockets on the front. No. 86324 would be renumbered 86424 and would go on to work for Rail Express Systems. It later passed to Network Rail and was painted yellow, but it was exported to Hungary as a source of spare parts for the Floyd fleet.

No. 86326, 31 July 1982

No. 86326 (E3195) is seen looking very respectable on one of the centre roads at Birmingham New Street. This was a great period for spending a few hours at New Street, with most trains transferring from diesel to electric haulage, and vice versa. No. 86326 would be renumbered 86426, and would be employed on parcels traffic. It would also be named *Pride of the Nation* when numbered 86426.

No. 86328, 9 March 1985

No. 86328 (E3159) *Aldaniti* is seen stabled at Bescot carrying BR blue livery. No. 86328 would be renumbered 86428 and then 86628 and is still in use today with Freightliner. 'Aldaniti' was the name of the racehorse that Bob Champion won the Grand National on in 1981.

No. 86329, 31 August 1984

No. 86329 (E3200) departs from Crewe with a southbound passenger working. This was later renumbered 86429, and would unfortunately be destroyed in the Colwich accident in 1986 along with No. 86211. No. 86329 was the last Class 86 to be built. It would be named *The Times* when numbered 86429.

No. 86401, 20 May 1987

No. 86401 (E3199) is seen passing through Adderley Park with a southbound InterCity working. The loco carries Network South East livery for use on Northampton workings and was the only member of the class so painted. It would later receive the name *Northampton Town*, and has since been preserved.

No. 86401, 10 June 1999

No. 86401 (E3199) *Hertfordshire Railtours* is seen on one of the through roads at Crewe. The loco carries EWS maroon livery and was one of just a handful to carry this livery, with EWS using them on parcels traffic. This was later preserved by the AC Locomotive Group.

No. 86401, 9 June 2007

No. 86401 (E3199) *Northampton Town* is seen at MOD Long Marston, having been superbly repainted back into Network South East livery. This was the only Class 86 to carry this livery. This loco was preserved by the AC Locomotive Group, and has since been returned to main-line use on the overnight Caledonian Sleeper trains.

No. 86401, 7 June 2009

No. 86401 (E3199) *Northampton Town* stands on display at MOD Long Marston carrying Network South East livery. This loco has since been repainted into Caledonian Sleeper livery to help out on such workings and is owned by the AC Locomotive Group.

No. 86406, 22 March 1986

No. 86406 (E3112) is seen at Crewe Works following classified overhaul, which included a repaint into original InterCity livery. This later passed to Freightliner and was renumbered 86606, but was scrapped in 2007.

No. 86406, 21 June 1989

No. 86406 (E3112) rests at Bescot carrying InterCity mainline livery. The addition of the red buffer beam and black headcode boxes certainly improved the appearance of the locos. Note as well as the multiple working cables and sockets. No. 86406 also carries the TDM cables for push-pull working and was later renumbered 86606.

No. 86408, 18 January 1986

No. 86408 (E3180) is seen arriving at Birmingham New Street with a passenger working. No. 86408 carries original InterCity livery and would go on to be renumbered 86501 following its bogies being re-geared. It has since reverted to 86608 and still works in the Freightliner fleet.

No. 86408, 22 March 1986

No. 86408 (E3180) is seen departing Crewe with a southbound passenger working. The loco carries original InterCity livery and is still in use today with Freightliner, although it now carries the number 86608.

Nos 86410 and 90041, 26 May 1990

No. 86410 (E3104) is seen piloting No. 90041 out of Crewe while on a passenger working. No. 86410 carries InterCity mainline livery, complete with small numbers, but was soon to be renumbered 86610. No. 90041 carries Railfreight Speedlink livery and both are still in regular use today with Freightliner.

No. 86416, 22 April 1987

No. 86416 (E3109) *Wigan Pier* is seen working south through Nuneaton with a passenger working. The loco carries original InterCity livery and would go on to work for Rail Express Systems before finally passing to EWS. It would be scrapped in 2005 by Booth Roe Metals, Rotherham.

No. 86416, 25 February 1993

No. 86416 (E3109) is seen stabled at Crewe while carrying Rail Express Systems livery. No. 86254, similarly liveried, is alongside, and at this time the parcels-allocated AC electrics could be found stabled at Crewe in between duties. No. 86416 would be scrapped by Booth Roe Metals, Rotherham, in 2005.

No. 86417, 29 October 1995

No. 86417 (E3146) is seen carrying Rail Express Systems livery while stabled at Polmadie, Glasgow. This was another EWS-operated Class 86 that was scrapped following the loss of parcels traffic, this being done by Booth Roe Metals, Rotherham, in 2004. This was once named *The Kingsman*.

No. 86417, 13 March 1997

No. 86417 (E3146) is seen working south through Thirsk, carrying Rail Express Systems livery with a matching rake of parcels vans. Class 86s were never common on the East Coast, this being one of their regular turns.

No. 86419, 21 August 1994

No. 86419 (E3120) is seen on display at Crewe Basford Hall open day, 1994. The loco carries Rail Express Systems livery and, following the loss of parcels traffic, it would be scrapped at Crewe Electric depot in 2003. This once carried the name *Post Haste – 150 Years of Travelling Post offices.*

No. 86420, 12 January 1985

No. 86420 (E3114) is seen stabled at Bescot carrying BR blue livery and still retains its cross-arm pantograph. This loco would go on to be renumbered 86620 and was used by Freightliner until it caught fire in 2007. It was later scrapped by Ron Hull Junior, Rotherham following the fire damage. This would go on to be named *Philip G Walton* when numbered 86620.

No. 86424, 20 April 2002

No.86424 (E3111) is seen at Birmingham International. The loco carries Rail Express Systems livery, was operated by EWS at the time and is seen on loan to Virgin Trains West Coast for passenger work. Note how the loco has lost the multiple working cables and sockets, which the holes where they were being plated over. This was later sold to Network Rail, who painted it yellow, but it was later sold to Floyd of Hungary for spare parts and duly exported.

No. 86425, 20 October 1993

No. 86425 (E3186) stands at Crewe with an empty stock move. The loco carries parcels red livery, and this batch of parcels-operated locos was regularly to be found on hire for passenger work; this practice still carrying on into EWS and Virgin Trains days. This was later named *Saint Mungo*. No. 86425 was later scrapped by Booth Roe Metals, Rotherham, in 2005.

No. 86426, 3 April 1985

No. 86426 (E3195) is seen carrying BR blue livery at Nuneaton while on a northbound passenger working. Note how the BR double arrow has been moved to under the secondman's window, and a new high-speed pantograph has been fitted. This loco would later be painted into a version of the original electric-blue livery. This was later named *Pride of the Nation*.

No. 86426, 29 March 1991

No. 86426 (E3195) arrives at Birmingham International with a West Coast working from London Euston to Wolverhampton. This loco carries InterCity mainline livery, but has the larger numbers rather than the tiny numbers.

No. 86426, 12 July 1992

No. 86426 (E3195) is seen on display at Doncaster Works open day, 1992. It had just been repainted into Rail Express Systems livery; this livery really suited the class. Doncaster Works has now mostly been demolished.

No. 86426, 13 January 1993

No. 86426 (E3195) is seen arriving at Crewe while on a CrossCountry passenger working. The parcels, based locos were regularly used by the InterCity department for passenger trains. No. 86426 would later be used by EWS, but was finally scrapped by Booth Roe Metals, Rotherham, in 2005.

No. 86426, 9 June 2002

No. 86426 (E3195) *Pride Of The Nation* is seen unusually stabled at Saltley. It was here for onward movement to Toton for repainting into Freightliner green livery as, despite being owned by EWS, it was going on long-term hire to Freightliner. AC electrics were extremely rare visitors to the diesel depot at Saltley, with the only other one I can recall being No. 92031, also following repainting at Toton.

No. 86427, 12 April 1986

No. 86427 (E3110) *The Industrial Society* is seen stabled at Bescot while still carrying original InterCity livery. Of note is the fact that it still retains the small headlight on the front, rather than the square headlight. This loco is still in use today with Freightliner, but has been renumbered 86627.

No. 86428, 18 October 1993

No. 86428 (E3159) *Aldaniti* is seen arriving at Crewe with an empty stock move, which consists of just two MK3 sleeper carriages. This loco had been renumbered 86628, but was temporarily renumbered back to 86428 following the reinstatement of the ETH equipment as it was on hire to the InterCity department. When the hire period finished, the ETH equipment was again isolated, and it became No. 86628 again. It is sill in use today with Freightliner.

No. 86430, 29 August 1989

No. 86430 (E3105) *Scottish National Orchestra* passes straight through Nuneaton while on a southbound passenger working. The loco carries original InterCity livery and still retains its multiple working cables and sockets, but also carries TDM cables, making the front end look a bit clustered. This also carried the name *Saint Edmund*.

No. 86430, 29 October 1995

No. 86430 (E3105) stands at Polmadie while carrying Rail Express Systems livery. By this time the multiple working sockets and cables had been removed. This was later painted Freightliner green as it went on long-term hire from EWS to Freightliner, but was finally scrapped by Booth Roe Metals, Rotherham, in 2005. This loco has carried the names *Scottish National Orchestra* and *Saint Edmund*.

Nos 86430 and 86401, 7 August 1996

No. 86430 (E3105) *Saint Edmund* leads classmate No. 86401 (E3199) through one of the through roads at Crewe while on a parcels working. Note that No. 86430 has lost its redundant headcode box by this time, the only one of the class to do so except for the ones exported to Hungary. Both locos carry Rail Express System livery.

No. 86431, 26 December 1989

No. 86431 (E3188) spends the Christmas period of 1989 stabled at Bescot. The loco carries InterCity mainline livery, complete with small running numbers. This loco was eventually renumbered 86631, but was scrapped following collision damage it received at Stafford while working with No. 86611.

No. 86431, 25 February 1993

No. 86431 (E3188) runs light engine through Crewe while carrying Railfreight Speedlink livery. This was one of a small number of Class 86/6s that went on hire to the InterCity department, having the ETH equipment reinstated, thus being renumbered back into the Class 86/4 series. When the hire period finished, the ETH equipment was isolated again, meaning they were renumbered back as Class 86/6s.

No. 86432, 27 October 1984

No. 86432 (E3148) is seen inside Crewe Works undergoing a classified overhaul. This overhaul included it being renumbered 86432 from 86032. It would later pass to Freightliner, and is still in use today numbered 86632. It also once carried the name *Brookside*.

No. 86501, 21 May 2000

No. 86501 (E3180) is seen on display at Crewe Works open day 2000. The loco had just been renumbered from 86608 following the fitment of re-geared bogies, and was the only loco so treated. It has since received a pair of ordinary bogies, and has been renumbered back to 86608. Note the *Crewe Basford Hall* name fitted, but covered up, although it would enter service without the name. The nameplate had come from loco No. 90135.

No. 86502, 2 June 1989

No. 86502 (E3131) *Lloyds List 250th Anniversary* is seen passing south through Nuneaton with a container working. This small sub class was renumbered from Class 86/2s for freight work, although they were only renumbered for a short time; No. 86502 was renumbered back to 86222 after only twelve months. The loco carries unbranded Railfreight livery, including a Willesden Greyhound depot plaque.

No. 86602, 16 June 2000

No. 86602 (E3170) is seen pausing at Carlisle while carrying Freightliner green livery. It is working in multiple with classmate No. 86605, which still carries Freightliner grey livery. No. 86602 was scrapped by Sandbach Car and Commercial Dismantlers in 2010.

No. 86604, 11 September 2005

No. 86604 (E3103) is seen on display at Crewe Works open day in 2005. No. 86604 carries Freightliner green livery and is still in use today with Freightliner.

No. 86604, 11 December 2012

No. 86604 (E3103) is seen pausing for a red signal at Milton Keynes Central while working a Freightliner service south along with classmate No. 86610. Both locos are still in use with Freightliner today.

Nos 86609 and 86638, 18 September 2012

No. 86609 (E3102) is seen passing through Nuneaton on the fast line along with classmate No. 86638. They are hauling No. 66571 dead in tow, and all three locos carry Freightliner green livery. No. 86609 is currently the oldest Class 86 left in service and is over fifty years old.

No. 86613, 30 October 2012

No. 86613 (E3128) is seen on one of the through roads at Crewe station. The loco carries Freightliner green and is one of sixteen still left in everyday use with Freightliner. These locos often run in pairs. This once carried the name *County of Lancashire*.

Nos 86614 and 86632, 29 March 1991

No. 86614 (E3145) *Frank Hornby* is seen working south through Birmingham International along with classmate No. 86632. Both locos carry Railfreight Speedlink livery and are seen on a container train. Nearly twenty-five years later, both locos are still in use with Freightliner on the same sort of workings.

No. 86614, 11 September 2005

No. 86614 (E3145) is seen stabled at Crewe Basford Hall while carrying Freightliner grey livery. This livery was used before Freightliner started painting its locos green. This once carried the name *Frank Hornby*.

No. 86620, 30 August 1992

No. 86620 (E3114) is seen on display at Bescot open day 1992. The loco carries Railfreight Speedlink livery and would later go on to be painted into Freightliner green livery. No. 86620 was withdrawn with fire damage and would be scrapped by Ron Hull Junior, Rotherham, in 2007. This later carried the name *Philip G Walton*.

No. 86620, 5 October 1993

No. 86620 (E3114) is seen passing through Crewe station at the head of the works test train. The loco carries Railfreight Speedlink livery. This was later named *Philip G Walton*.

No. 86623, 26 July 1996

No. 86623 (E3152) works north through Tamworth, carrying Freightliner grey livery along, with classmate No. 86637. No. 86623 was later scrapped by Sandbach Car and Commercial Dismantlers at Crewe L&NWR in 2010, meanwhile No. 86637 is still in service with Freightliner.

No. 86623, 21 May 2000

No. 86623 (E3152) stands at Crewe Basford Hall on the day of the nearby works open day. No. 86623 wears Freightliner grey livery and was scrapped ten years later at Crewe L&NWR.

No. 86627, 26 July 1996

No. 86627 (E3110) *The Industrial Society* passes south through Tamworth, carrying unbranded Railfreight livery. The loco is on a very short Freightliner working, and it was unusual to get a Class 86/6 running singularly. No. 86627 is still in use with Freightliner today.

No. 86627, 30 October 2012

No. 86627 (E3110) is seen at Crewe carrying Freightliner green livery, although it looks a bit scruffy with part of the transfer missing. This once carried the name *The Industrial Society*.

No. 86631, 30 August 1998

No. 86631 (E3188) is seen on display at the Toton open day 1998. The loco carries green Freightliner livery, which also includes the logo above the cab window, a feature not too many locos carried. No. 86631 would be withdrawn following collision damage it received at Stafford while working with No. 86611. Both locos would be scrapped at Crewe Works in 2005 by Harry Needle.

No. 86631, 21 May 2000

No. 86631 (E3188) is seen on display inside Crewe Works during the 2000 open day. The loco carries Freightliner green livery and is hooked up to the overhead crane.

No. 86632, 27 March 1993

No. 86632 (E3148) *Brookside* is seen inside the repair shed at Crewe Electric depot while undergoing repairs. The loco carries Railfreight Speedlink livery and would later pass to Freightliner. Some of these locos have carried many different running numbers over the years, including No. 86632, which has carried 86032, 86432 and 86632. This loco is still in use today with Freightliner.

No. 86633, 26 July 1990

No. 86633 (E3198) *Wulfruna* is seen stabled at Crewe while carrying Railfreight Speedlink livery. The loco has the addition of a red buffer beam, which certainly makes a difference. This loco passed to Freightliner, but was scrapped at Crewe L&NWR in 2013. Wulfruna was a Saxon noblewoman who lived over a thousand years ago.

No. 86634, 15 April 1993

No. 86634 (E3187) *University of London* is seen stabled at Crewe, having not long been repainted into Railfreight Speedlink livery. The loco also carries a Crewe Electric Eagle depot plaque. This was scrapped by Booth Roe Metals, Rotherham, in 2005.

No. 86635, 20 August 1993

No. 86635 (E3124) is seen parked round the back of Crewe station. The loco has just been released from overhaul, including a repaint into Railfreight Speedlink livery. The loco would eventually be painted into Freightliner green livery, but was withdrawn and scrapped at Crewe L&NWR in 2013 by Sandbach Car & Commercial Dismantlers.

No. 86637, 30 October 2012

No. 86637 (E3130) is seen on one of the through roads at Crewe, wearing the latest Freightliner PowerHaul livery, and is one of two locos painted in this livery.

No. 86637, 20 May 2014

No. 86637 (E3130) works north through Rugeley Trent Valley along with classmate No. 86638. No. 86637 carries the latest Freightliner PowerHaul livery. They are seen on a Tilbury to Crewe Freightliner working.

No. 86701, 30 October 2012

No. 86701 (E3129) *Orion* is seen stabled at Rugby wearing Colas Rail Freight livery, the only Class 86 to carry these colours. It was owned by Electric Traction Limited, but was on hire to Colas and was being used with a rake of former Great Western Motorail vans as a trial for TNT. No. 86701 was renumbered from 86205 and has since been sold for spare parts ready for export to Bulgaria. This carried the name *City of Lancaster* when numbered 86205.

No. 86701, 7 June 2014

No. 86701 (E3129) *Orion* is seen stabled at Rugby wearing Colas Rail Freight livery. This was renumbered from 86205 when it was overhauled for Electric Traction Limited, who hired it out to Colas. This loco is expected to be exported to Bulgaria as a source of spare parts for the AC electric fleet in use over there. As No. 86205 this was named *City of Lancaster*.

No. 86901, 16 January 2007

No. 86901 (E3136) *Chief Engineer* is seen stabled at Rugby. This had been taken over by Network Rail and was one of two Class 86s converted to mobile load bank locos. No. 86901 was converted from 86253, and is currently stored at C.F. Booths, Rotherham, for spare parts recovery before final scrapping. This was named *The Manchester Guardian* when numbered 86253.

No. 86902, 11 April 2005

No. 86902 (E3190) *Rail Vehicle Engineering* is seen at Rugby not long after being converted to a mobile load bank loco by Network Rail. This had been converted from 86210 and is currently is store at C.F. Booths, Rotherham, for spare parts recovery before final scrapping. This once carried the name *City of Edinburgh* when numbered 86210.

No. 86902, 7 February 2009

No. 86902 (E3190) *Rail Vehicle Engineering* is seen stabled on one of the centre roads at Carlisle carrying Network Rail yellow livery. This had been converted from 86210 into a mobile load bank loco and is currently in storage at C.F. Booths, Rotherham. As No. 86210 this was named *City of Edinburgh*.

E3138, 1966

E3138 (No. 86242) is seen waiting to depart from London Euston in original condition. The Class 86s really suited the early electric blue livery, and E3138 is seen surrounded by BR blue-and-grey MK2 carriages. E3138 was later renumbered 86242 under TOPS, and has since been exported to Hungary, working for Floyd. This loco once carried the names *James Kennedy G.C.*, and *Colchester Castle.*